conte

CW00369589

British & North American Readers:
Please note that Australian cup and
spoon measurements are metric. A quick
conversion guide appears on page 63.
A glossary explaining unfamiliar terms
and ingredients begins on page 60.

2   fighting fat

Eating less fat (and less saturated fat, in particular) is one of the best things you can do for your health and your body shape. You don't have to give up fat altogether — just reduce your intake.

A small amount of fat is essential for good health, vitality and clear skin. Children, especially, need some fat in their meals to grow and develop properly. A low-fat diet is not recommended for children under the age of five.

How much fat do I need?

Women: the recommended intake of fat is 50 to 60 grams a day for moderately active women aged 18 to 54 years. Very active women can eat 70 to 80 grams a day.

Men: men should also aim for 70 to 80 grams a day if they are fairly active, or 80 to 100 grams if they do a lot of physical activity.

To lose weight

Keep your fat intake to 30 to 50 grams a day. To find out how much fat is in food, buy a fat counter booklet, available at newsagents and some chemists.

Facts about fat

• 'Light' on a label doesn't necessarily mean the food is low in fat. Light potato crisps are lightly salted and thinly sliced, but contain the same amount of fat as other crisps. Light olive oil has a lighter flavour, but the same amount of fat as regular olive oil.

• Cholesterol is found only in animal products. So food made from plants is automatically free of cholesterol, and labelling it as 'cholesterol-free' is simply a marketing ploy.

• Kilojoules are the metric equivalent of calories. To convert (roughly) to calories, divide kilojoules by 4. For example, a slice of bread at 250 kilojoules is equivalent to 60 calories.

150 ml skim milk = 0.03g fat
200g low-fat yogurt = 0.4g fat
200g ricotta = 18g fat
200g cheddar = 13.3g fat

THE FATS WE EAT

NEGLIGIBLE

virtually no fat

baked beans
crabs, lobsters,
  prawns, cooked
  without fat
fruit, fresh,
  canned, stewed
  or dried
legumes (dried
  beans, peas,
  lentils)
noodles, boiled
  (not instant)
pasta, boiled
potatoes, boiled,
  or baked in jacket
rice, white,
  steamed or boiled
skim milk
sugar, honey,
  golden syrup
vegetables, raw,
  steamed, boiled
  or dry-baked
  (except for olives
  and avocados)
yeast spreads

LOW

*less than 3 per
  cent fat*

bread, all varieties
breakfast cereals
  (excluding muesli)
crispbreads
fish, white, grilled
  or steamed
low-fat and
  reduced-fat milk
low-fat soy
  beverages
muffins, crumpets
oats, rolled
  (porridge)
oysters, scallops,
  squid
rice, brown,
  steamed or boiled
yogurt, low-fat

MEDIUM

3 to 20 per cent fat

cottage cheese
egg yolks
fillo pastry
fish fingers, fried
full-cream milk,
  goats milk
lean beef, veal,

trim lamb,
  chicken, new-
  fashioned pork
  (grilled or cooked
  without fat)
muesli, Swiss-style
muesli, toasted
olives
potatoes, mashed
  with milk and
  butter
rice bran
salmon, tuna, fresh
  (grilled or
  steamed) and
  canned
salmon, smoked
sardines, canned
  in oil
soy beverages
venison, kangaroo
  and other game
  meat, cooked
  without fat
wheat bran, oat
  bran

HIGH

*21 to 50 per cent
  fat*

avocados
bacon, pan-fried
cheese, hard,
  cream cheese
chocolate
coconut cream,
  coconut milk
corn chips
cream
delicatessen
  meats, salami
doughnuts
fried food,
  crumbed chicken,
  fried fish pieces
fried rice
sausages, rissoles,
  fatty meat

VERY HIGH

over 50 per cent fat

butter
margarine
nuts
oils, all types,
  including light oils
peanut butter, nut
  butter
seeds (sesame,
  sunflower)

400g small mussels

16 medium uncooked prawns (400g)

1 teaspoon olive oil

2 large brown onions (400g), sliced

4 cloves garlic, crushed

1/4 cup (60ml) dry white wine

1/4 cup (60ml) tomato paste

2 x 400g cans tomatoes

1/3 cup (80ml) water

500g spinach fettuccine

1/3 cup (80ml) buttermilk

400g seafood marinara mix

2 tablespoons chopped fresh basil leaves

2 tablespoons chopped fresh parsley

Scrub mussels, remove beards. Shell and devein prawns, leaving tails intact.

Heat oil in large non-stick pan; cook onion and garlic, stirring, until onion is soft. Stir in wine and tomato paste; bring to boil. Add undrained crushed tomatoes and water; simmer, uncovered, about 10 minutes or until sauce has thickened slightly.

Cook pasta in large pan of boiling water, uncovered, until just tender; drain.

Stir buttermilk and all seafood into tomato mixture; simmer, covered, until seafood is just cooked, stirring occasionally. Stir in herbs. Gently **toss** seafood sauce through hot pasta.

Per serving fat 5.9g; kJ 2558

chicken
yakitori

4 chicken breast fillets (680g), sliced

1/2 cup (125ml) bottled teriyaki marinade

2 cloves garlic, crushed

2 teaspoons grated fresh ginger

1 teaspoon sugar

cooking oil spray

dipping sauce

1/4 cup (60ml) soy sauce

1 tablespoon sweet chilli sauce

1 green onion, sliced thinly

Per serving fat 4.8g; kJ 1032

Combine chicken with teriyaki marinade, garlic, ginger and sugar in bowl. Cover; refrigerate 10 minutes. Drain chicken over medium bowl; reserve marinade.
Thread chicken onto 16 skewers. Cook skewers on heated oiled grill plate (or grill or barbecue) until browned all over and cooked through, brushing with reserved marinade mixture occasionally during cooking. Serve skewers with Dipping Sauce.
Dipping Sauce Combine all ingredients in small bowl.

beef and black bean
stir-fry

1 teaspoon peanut oil

400g beef rump steak, sliced thinly

1 clove garlic, crushed

1 medium brown onion (150g), sliced

2 celery sticks (150g), sliced

1 teaspoon cornflour

1/4 cup (60ml) black bean sauce

1 teaspoon teriyaki sauce

Heat oil in large non-stick pan; stir-fry beef, in batches, until browned all over.

Cook garlic, onion and celery in same pan, stirring, until onion is soft and golden.

Return beef to pan with blended cornflour and sauces, stir over heat until sauce boils and thickens.

Per serving fat 4.3g; kJ 691

8

stir-fried
mexican beef

750g beef eye fillet steaks, sliced thinly

35g packet taco seasoning

cooking oil spray

1 large red onion (300g), sliced

1 medium red capsicum (200g), sliced thinly

1 medium yellow capsicum (200g), sliced thinly

4 small tomatoes (520g), seeded, sliced

2 tablespoons chopped fresh coriander leaves

Combine beef and seasoning in bowl. Coat large non-stick pan with cooking oil spray, heat pan; cook beef and onion, in batches, until beef is browned all over.

Cook capsicum in same pan, stirring, until tender. Return beef and onion to pan with tomato and coriander; cook, stirring, until hot.

Per serving fat 9.3g; kJ 1366

chilli calamari
salad

4 medium calamari
hoods (800g)

1 teaspoon olive oil

2 cloves garlic,
crushed

$1/2$ teaspoon sambal
oelek

$1/2$ teaspoon coarsely
ground black pepper

1 tablespoon balsamic
vinegar

2 teaspoons white
wine vinegar

1 teaspoon sugar

200g mesclun

Cut calamari hoods open, cut shallow diagonal slashes in criss-cross
pattern on inside surface; cut into 6cm pieces.
Heat oil in large non-stick pan; cook combined calamari, garlic, sambal
oelek and pepper, in batches, until browned all over and just tender.
Return calamari to pan with combined vinegars and sugar; stir until hot.
Serve calamari mixture with mesclun.

Per serving fat 3.8g; kJ 756

10 spicy chicken
fried rice

You will need to cook 2 cups (400g) white long-grain rice for this recipe.

cooking oil spray

2 eggs, beaten lightly

5 chicken thigh fillets (550g), chopped

2 medium brown onions (300g), sliced

1 tablespoon ground cumin

2 teaspoons ground coriander

1 teaspoon ground cinnamon

2 small fresh red chillies, seeded, chopped finely

2 cloves garlic, crushed

1 large red capsicum (350), sliced

115g baby corn, chopped

6 cups cooked white rice

4 green onions, sliced

2 tablespoons ketjap manis

2 tablespoons coarsely chopped fresh coriander leaves

Coat large non-stick pan with cooking oil spray, heat pan, add half the egg, swirl so egg forms a thin omelette; cook until set. Transfer omelette to board, roll, cut into thin strips. Repeat.

Cook chicken and onion in same pan, stirring, until browned all over and chicken is cooked through, remove from pan. Add spices, chilli and garlic to same pan; cook, stirring, until fragrant. Add capsicum and corn; cook, stirring, until tender. Return chicken mixture to pan with omelette strips and remaining ingredients; cook, stirring, until hot.

Per serving fat 10.3g; kJ 2585

12 mediterranean lamb burgers

5 lamb fillets (400g), chopped

1 egg white

1 cup (70g) stale wholemeal breadcrumbs

1 tablespoon fresh rosemary sprigs

1/4 cup loosely packed fresh mint leaves

1 teaspoon grated lemon rind

2 cloves garlic, quartered

1 tablespoon tomato paste

4 cos lettuce leaves, halved

1 large tomato (250g), sliced

1/2 small red onion (50g), sliced

4 wholemeal bread rolls

yogurt sauce

2/3 cup (160ml) low-fat yogurt

1 clove garlic, crushed

1 tablespoon finely chopped fresh mint leaves

1/2 Lebanese cucumber (65g), seeded, chopped

Per serving fat 6g; kJ1540

Process lamb, egg white, breadcrumbs, herbs, rind, garlic and paste until smooth. Shape mixture into 4 patties, using damp hands. Cook patties in large heated non-stick pan until browned both sides and cooked through. Layer lettuce leaves, patties, Yogurt Sauce, tomato and onion on bread rolls.

Yogurt Sauce Combine all ingredients in bowl.

char-grilled

chicken with warm tomato salad

4 chicken breast fillets (680g)

2 tablespoons lime juice

1/4 cup (60ml) sweet chilli sauce

2 cloves garlic, crushed

cooking oil spray

3 green onions, chopped

warm tomato salad

2 medium brown onions (300g), halved, sliced

2 tablespoons water

1/4 cup (55g) sugar

2 tablespoons red wine vinegar

2 tablespoons sweet chilli sauce

1/4 cup (60ml) water, extra

1/4 cup (60ml) orange juice

1 fresh green jalapeno pepper, sliced

8 medium (600g) egg tomatoes, sliced

Combine chicken, juice, sauce and garlic in large bowl. Cover; refrigerate 10 minutes. Drain chicken; discard marinade.

Cook chicken on heated oiled grill plate (or grill or barbecue) until browned both sides and cooked through. Serve chicken with Warm Tomato Salad, top with green onion.

Warm Tomato Salad Cook onion in the water in large non-stick pan; stirring, until onion is very soft. Add sugar; cook, stirring, 1 minute. Add vinegar; simmer, uncovered, 1 minute. Stir in sauce, extra water and juice; simmer, uncovered, 3 minutes. Add remaining ingredients; stir gently until heated through.

Per serving fat 5.6g; kJ 1377

14 indian **spiced**
beef and pumpkin

cooking oil spray

400g pumpkin, peeled, sliced thinly

750g beef rump steak, sliced thinly

1 medium brown onion (150g), sliced thinly

2 cloves garlic, crushed

1 tablespoon grated fresh ginger

$1/2$ teaspoon ground cinnamon

2 teaspoons ground cumin

2 teaspoons ground coriander

1 tablespoon ground turmeric

1 teaspoon sweet paprika

200g baby spinach leaves

Coat large non-stick pan with cooking oil spray, heat pan; cook pumpkin, in batches, until browned all over and tender.

Cook combined beef, onion, garlic and spices, in batches, until beef is browned all over. Return beef mixture to pan with pumpkin and spinach; cook, stirring, until spinach is just wilted.

Per serving fat 6.6g; kJ 1271

lamb fillets

with tomato mint raita

2 teaspoons ground cumin

2 teaspoons ground coriander

1 clove garlic, crushed

1¹/₂ cups (375ml) low-fat yogurt

9 lamb fillets (720g)

cooking oil spray

2 small tomatoes (260g), seeded, chopped finely

1 tablespoon finely shredded mint leaves

1 tablespoon lemon juice

Per serving fat 8g; kJ1226

Combine cumin, coriander, garlic and half the yogurt in large bowl; add lamb, coat with yogurt mixture.
Cook lamb on heated oiled grill plate (or grill or barbecue) until browned all over and cooked as desired, brushing with yogurt mixture occasionally.
Meanwhile, combine remaining yogurt, tomato, mint and juice in small bowl. Slice lamb; serve topped with tomato mint raita.

spinach omelette
with stir-fried vegetables

4 eggs, separated
1/2 cup (40g) finely chopped spinach
4 egg whites
cooking oil spray
stir-fried vegetables
2 tablespoons water
1 medium brown onion (150g), chopped finely
1 clove garlic, crushed
1 medium red capsicum (200g), sliced thinly
100g snow peas, halved
2 baby bok choy (300g), chopped
2 choy sum (300g), chopped
1 1/4 cups (100g) bean sprouts
1 tablespoon ketjap manis

Combine beaten egg yolks and spinach in bowl. Beat all egg whites in small bowl with electric mixer until soft peaks form. Fold egg whites into spinach mixture in 2 batches. Coat non-stick pan (base measure 24cm) with cooking oil spray, heat pan; spread half the mixture into pan. Cook until browned underneath. Cover handle with foil, place pan under grill until top is just set. Top with half the Stir-Fried Vegetables, fold, slide omelette onto board. Cut omelette in half. Repeat.
Stir-Fried Vegetables Heat water in large non-stick pan; cook onion and garlic, stirring, until onion is soft. Add capsicum; cook, stirring, until tender. Add remaining ingredients; cook, stirring, until just wilted.

Per serving fat 6.7g; kJ 624

18 mixed vegetable and lentil curry

1 teaspoon vegetable oil

1 medium brown onion (150g), chopped

2 tablespoons mild curry powder

2 tablespoons coconut milk powder

1/2 cup (125ml) warm water

1 litre (4 cups) vegetable stock

1 cup (200g) brown lentils

1 medium carrot (120g), chopped

600g cauliflower, chopped

300g butter beans

200g baby green beans

2 tablespoons chopped fresh basil leaves

1/2 cup (125ml) low-fat yogurt

1/4 teaspoon ground cumin

Heat oil in large non-stick pan; cook onion and curry powder, stirring, until onion is soft. Add blended coconut milk powder and water, then stock and lentils; simmer, covered, 20 minutes. **Add** carrot and cauliflower; simmer, covered, 10 minutes. Stir in beans; simmer, covered, about 5 minutes or until vegetables are tender. Stir in basil. Top with yogurt and cumin.

Per serving fat 11.8g; kJ 1465

red wine sauce and polenta

*4 beef eye fillet steaks
(600g)*

*³/₄ cup (180ml) dry red
wine*

*¹/₃ cup (80ml)
redcurrant jelly*

*1.125 litres (4¹/₂ cups)
chicken stock*

*1¹/₂ cups (255g)
polenta*

*¹/₂ cup (40g) grated
parmesan cheese*

Per serving fat 11.4g;
kJ 2466

Cook beef in large heated non-stick pan, until browned both sides and
cooked as desired.

Remove from pan, cover to keep warm. Add wine and jelly to pan;
simmer, uncovered, until thickened slightly.

Meanwhile, bring stock to boil in large pan, add polenta; simmer, stirring,
about 5 minutes or until polenta thickens. Stir in cheese. Serve steaks
with sauce and polenta.

20 spring vegetable soup

2 teaspoons vegetable oil

1 large brown onion (200g), chopped

2 cloves garlic, crushed

1 medium leek (350g), sliced

2 medium carrots (240g), sliced

2 celery sticks (150g), sliced

200g mushrooms, chopped

1.25 litres (6 cups) vegetable stock

50g spaghettini

1 tablespoon finely chopped
fresh parsley

Heat oil in large pan; cook onion and garlic, stirring, until onion is soft. Add leek, carrot and celery; cook, stirring, until vegetables are soft. Add mushrooms; cook, stirring, 1 minute. Stir in stock; simmer, uncovered, 15 minutes. **Add** pasta; simmer, uncovered, until just tender. Stir in parsley.

Per serving fat 5.4g; kJ 711

beef with

capers and anchovies

1 teaspoon olive oil

500g beef rump steak, sliced thinly

2 cloves garlic, crushed

2 medium red onions (340g), sliced

4 anchovy fillets, drained, chopped

1 tablespoon drained capers, chopped

2 tablespoons balsamic vinegar

1/4 cup (35g) pimiento-stuffed green
olives, sliced

2 tablespoons shredded fresh basil leaves

Per serving fat 5.6g; kJ 828

Heat oil in large non-stick pan; cook combined beef and garlic, in batches, until browned all over. Cook onion in same pan, stirring, until soft and tender.

Return beef to pan with anchovies, capers and vinegar; cook, stirring, until hot. Stir in olives and shredded basil.

warm lamb

2 tablespoons chopped fresh mint leaves

1 teaspoon hot paprika

$1/2$ teaspoon ground cumin

2 teaspoons grated lime rind

$2/3$ cup (160ml) low-fat yogurt

1 Lebanese cucumber (130g)

5 lamb fillets (400g), halved

1 tablespoon Dijon mustard

2 tablespoons chopped fresh rosemary

1 tablespoon chopped fresh marjoram

1 teaspoon coarsely ground black pepper

2 small tomatoes (260g), seeded, sliced

150g mesclun

Combine half the mint and half the paprika with the cumin, rind and yogurt in bowl.
Slice cucumber thinly lengthways, using a vegetable peeler.
Brush lamb with mustard, roll in combined rosemary, marjoram, pepper and remaining mint and paprika. Cook lamb, in batches, in large heated non-stick pan until browned all over and cooked as desired. Slice lamb thinly. Return to pan with tomato; cook, stirring, until hot.
Serve lamb with cucumber and mesclun, drizzled with yogurt mixture.

Per serving fat 4.2g; kJ 700

24 fettuccine with rolled omelette and vegetables

250g fettuccine

1 teaspoon peanut oil

4 eggs, beaten lightly

500g asparagus, chopped

150g snow peas, sliced

2 tablespoons soy sauce

2 tablespoons oyster sauce

2 tablespoons sweet chilli sauce

Per serving fat 8g; kJ 1501

Cook pasta in large pan of boiling water, uncovered, until just tender; drain and set aside.

Meanwhile, heat oil in large non-stick pan; cook eggs, swirling, to form thin omelette. Remove omelette from pan. Roll omelette tightly; slice into rounds. Cover to keep warm.

Cook asparagus in same pan until almost tender. Add snow peas and combined sauces; cook, covered, about 1 minute or until vegetables are just tender. Gently toss pasta and omelette rounds with vegetables until heated through.

veal

pizzaiola

2 teaspoons olive oil

1 clove garlic, crushed

2 tablespoons dry
white wine

1 tablespoon chopped
fresh oregano

$^1/_2$ cup (125ml) beef
stock

3 cups (750ml) bottled
chunky tomato pasta
sauce

$^2/_3$ cup (80g) small
black olives

4 veal steaks (500g)

Per serving 7g; kJ1250

To make sauce, heat non-stick pan with half the oil. Add garlic, wine and oregano; simmer, uncovered, until reduced by half. Add stock and sauce; simmer, uncovered, about 10 minutes or until sauce thickens slightly. Stir in olives.

Heat remaining oil in large non-stick pan; cook veal, until browned both sides and cooked as desired. Serve veal with sauce.

26 tomato, bean and pasta soup

³/₄ cup (135g) wholemeal pasta spirals
1 large brown onion (200g), chopped
1 litre (4 cups) chicken stock
2 cups (500ml) bottled tomato pasta sauce
1 teaspoons chopped fresh oregano
440g can 4-bean mix, rinsed, drained
2 medium zucchini (240g), chopped
2 tablespoons chopped fresh parsley

Cook pasta in large pan of boiling water, uncovered, until just tender; drain.

Combine onion with 2 tablespoons of the stock in large pan; cook, stirring, until onion is soft. Add remaining stock, sauce and oregano; boil, uncovered, 15 minutes. Add beans and zucchini; simmer, uncovered, 10 minutes. Stir in pasta and parsley; heat.

Per serving
fat 1.6g; kJ 850

pork steaks

with spicy barbecue sauce

cooking oil spray
4 pork leg schnitzels (400g)
400g can tomatoes
1 tablespoon brown vinegar
2 teaspoons Worcestershire sauce
1/2 teaspoon Tabasco sauce
2 tablespoons brown sugar

Coat large non-stick pan with cooking oil spray, heat pan; cook pork until browned both sides and cooked through. Remove from pan, cover to keep warm.
Add undrained crushed tomatoes and remaining ingredients to same pan; simmer, uncovered, until thickened. Serve sauce with pork.

Per serving fat 5.7g; kJ 950

28 risoni, lamb and silverbeet
soup

¹/₂ cup (110g) risoni
1 large red capsicum (350g)
cooking oil spray
4 lamb fillets (320g), sliced thinly
¹/₂ cup (125ml) water
1 small leek (200g), sliced
2 cloves garlic, crushed
1 teaspoon chopped fresh rosemary
1 tablespoon tomato paste
1¹/₂ cups (375ml) vegetable stock
1.5 litres (6 cups) water, extra
1 chicken stock cube
1 small zucchini (90g), halved, sliced
4 silverbeet leaves (320g), shredded

Cook pasta in medium pan of boiling water, uncovered, until just tender; drain and set aside.

Quarter capsicum, remove seeds and membranes. Roast under grill or in very hot oven, skin side up, until skin blisters and blackens. Cover capsicum pieces in plastic or paper for 5 minutes, peel away skin, cut into 1cm strips.

Coat large non-stick pan with cooking oil spray, heat pan; cook lamb, in batches, until browned all over.

Add water, leek, garlic and rosemary to same pan; simmer, uncovered, until almost all the water has evaporated. Add paste, stock, extra water and crumbled stock cube; boil, uncovered, 15 minutes.

Return lamb to pan with zucchini; simmer, covered, until zucchini is just tender. Add silverbeet, pasta and capsicum; stir until silverbeet is wilted.

Per serving fat 4.5g; kJ 926

30 sweet and sour chicken

1 teaspoon peanut oil
5 chicken tenderloins (375g)
2 cloves garlic, crushed
2 teaspoons grated fresh ginger
250g mushrooms, chopped
1 small pineapple (800g), peeled, chopped
3 teaspoons cornflour
³/₄ cup (180ml) chicken stock
1 tablespoon soy sauce
¹/₄ cup (60ml) tomato sauce
2 tablespoons brown vinegar
1 tablespoon brown sugar
80g snow pea sprouts

Per serving fat 5.6g; kJ 964

Heat oil in large non-stick pan; cook combined chicken, garlic and ginger, in batches, until browned all over and chicken is cooked through.
Cook mushrooms in same pan, stirring, 2 minutes. Add pineapple, blended cornflour and stock, sauces, vinegar and sugar; stir over heat until sauce boils and thickens.
Return chicken to pan with sprouts; stir until hot.

pork

and chilli pasta

375g penne

cooking oil spray

2 pork fillets (500g), sliced

1 small brown onion (80g), chopped

1 clove garlic, crushed

2 x 400g cans tomatoes

1/4 cup (60ml) water

2 tablespoons tomato paste

1 1/2 tablespoons sweet chilli sauce

2 teaspoons sugar

1 teaspoon dried basil

1/2 cup (60g) black olives, seeded, halved

Cook pasta in large pan of boiling water, uncovered, until just tender; drain.
Coat large non-stick pan with cooking oil spray, heat pan; cook pork, in batches, until browned all over.
Cook onion and garlic in same pan, stirring, until onion is soft. Add undrained crushed tomatoes, water, paste, sauce, sugar, basil and olives; simmer, uncovered, until thickened slightly. Return pork to pan with pasta; stir over heat until hot.

Per serving fat 7.7g; kJ 2276

stir-fried asian greens

500g asparagus, trimmed

1 medium brown onion (150g)

1 clove garlic, crushed

200g baby bok choy, trimmed

200g baby tat soi, trimmed

1 tablespoon sweet soy sauce

2 tablespoons water

Cut asparagus in half. Cut onion into thin wedges. Heat oiled wok or large pan; stir-fry onion and garlic until onion is just soft. Add asparagus; stir-fry until almost tender. Add bok choy and tat soi; stir-fry 2 minutes. Stir in combined sauce and water, stir until tat soi is just wilted.

Per serving fat 0.4g; kJ 158

Vegetables are naturally low in fat, but steamed vegies on their own are also low in interest. Add some garlic, a few nuts, some soy sauce or maple syrup, and your low-fat vegetables turn into a treat.

roasted baby vegetables in maple syrup

1kg baby new potatoes, halved

400g baby carrots, peeled

500g baby turnips

500g baby beetroot

1 tablespoon seeded mustard

1/3 cup (80ml) maple syrup

1 teaspoon cracked black pepper

2 cloves garlic, crushed

From top: Pan-fried lemon vegetables; Stir-fried Asian greens; Roasted baby vegetables in maple syrup.

Place vegetables in baking dish, pour over combined mustard, syrup, pepper and garlic; shake pan to coat vegetables with maple mixture.

Bake, uncovered, in very hot oven about 40 minutes or until vegetables are soft and lightly browned, stirring occasionally.

Per serving fat 0.7g; kJ 1347

pan-fried lemon vegetables

500g baby potatoes

3 medium zucchini (360g), sliced

125g button mushrooms, sliced

olive oil spray

3 cloves garlic

2 tablespoons chopped fresh flat-leaf parsley

2 teaspoons grated lemon rind

Boil potatoes 2 minutes, stand 5 minutes; drain. Cut into 1cm slices. Add zucchini to pan of boiling water, return to boil; drain.
Spray non-stick pan with oil, add potatoes, fry 2 minutes, turning once, add mushrooms, cook 2 minutes. Add zucchini parsley, garlic and rind. Toss until heated through.

Per serving fat 1.3g; kJ 451

marinated tofu and bok choy
stir-fry

350g firm tofu

1 teaspoon peanut oil

1 large brown onion
(200g), sliced

1 medium red
capsicum (200g),
sliced thinly

200g snow peas

1/4 cup (60ml)
vegetable stock

400g bok choy,
shredded

420g thin fresh egg
noodles

marinade

1/4 cup (60ml) hoi sin
sauce

1/4 cup (60ml) oyster
sauce

1 tablespoon soy
sauce

1 teaspoon grated
fresh ginger

2 cloves garlic,
crushed

Cut tofu into 2cm cubes; combine tofu and
Marinade in bowl. Cover; refrigerate 10 minutes.
Heat oil in large non-stick pan; cook onion and
capsicum, stirring, until tender. Add peas and
stock; cook, stirring until hot. Add bok choy,
noodles and undrained tofu to pan; stir gently
until hot.
Marinade Combine all ingredients in bowl.

Per serving fat 7.9g;
kJ 1459

snow peas and asparagus

10g butter

2 cloves garlic, crushed

4 veal steaks (500g)

4 green onions, sliced

250g asparagus, chopped

200g snow peas

250g cherry tomatoes

2 teaspoons cornflour

1/2 cup (125ml) chicken stock

Heat butter in large non-stick pan; cook garlic and veal until browned both sides and cooked as desired. Remove veal from pan, cover to keep warm.
Cook onion, asparagus, snow peas and tomatoes in same pan, stirring, 1 minute. Stir in blended cornflour and stock; stir over heat until mixture boils and thickens slightly. Serve vegetable mixture over veal.

Per serving fat 4.3g; kJ 801

prawns and vegetables
with noodles

450g Hokkien noodles

16 large uncooked prawns (800g)

1 teaspoon peanut oil

3 cloves garlic, crushed

1 teaspoon finely chopped fresh ginger

1 large red capsicum (350g), sliced

200g oyster mushrooms, halved

3 cups (240g) shredded Chinese cabbage

360g Chinese broccoli, shredded

1 cup (80g) bean sprouts

1 teaspoon coarsely ground black pepper

1 tablespoon rice vinegar

2 tablespoons oyster sauce

1 tablespoon light soy sauce

2 tablespoons chopped fresh garlic chives

Rinse noodles in hot water; drain and set aside. Shell and devein prawns, leaving tails intact.

Heat oil in large non-stick pan; cook garlic, ginger, capsicum, mushrooms and prawns, stirring, until prawns just change colour. Add noodles, vegetables and combined remaining ingredients; cook, stirring, until cabbage is just wilted.

Per serving fat 3.5g; kJ 1312

38   cajun chicken
with lime, tomato and avocado

2 medium limes (160g)

6 medium egg tomatoes (450g)

cooking oil spray

1 medium avocado (250g), peeled, sliced

2 tablespoons coarsely chopped fresh coriander leaves

4 chicken breast fillets (680g)

2 tablespoons Cajun seasoning

Per serving fat 15.4g; kJ 1363

Cut limes and tomatoes into wedges. Cook lime and tomato on heated oiled grill plate (or grill or barbecue) until browned both sides. Combine lime and tomato in small bowl with avocado and coriander.

Coat chicken with seasoning; cook on heated oiled grill plate (or grill or barbecue) until browned both sides and cooked through. Slice chicken and serve with lime mixture.

soy and chilli
fish parcels

4 white fish fillets
(600g)

cooking oil spray

1¹/₂ cups (120g) bean
sprouts

3 cloves garlic,
crushed

4 green onions, sliced

¹/₄ teaspoon sesame
oil

2 tablespoons ketjap
manis

1 large fresh red chilli,
seeded, chopped

2 teaspoons sweet
sherry

Per serving fat 5.8g; kJ 813

Divide fish among 4 large pieces of foil which have been coated lightly with cooking oil spray. Divide sprouts among fish, top with combined remaining ingredients.

Seal foil to enclose fish; transfer to baking dish. Bake in moderate oven about 30 minutes or until fish is just cooked through.

chilli octopus with fettuccine

1kg baby octopus

2 tablespoons mango chutney

$^1/_3$ cup (80ml) lemon juice

$^1/_4$ cup (60ml) bottled no-oil French dressing

2 cloves garlic, crushed

2 tablespoons honey

2 tablespoons chopped fresh coriander leaves

4 green onions, chopped

500g fettuccine

1 teaspoon vegetable oil

2 tablespoons chopped fresh parsley

Remove and discard heads and beaks from octopus. Combine octopus, chutney, juice, dressing, garlic, honey, coriander and onion in bowl. Cover; refrigerate 10 minutes.

Drain octopus over medium bowl; reserve the marinade.

Cook pasta in large pan of boiling water, uncovered, until just tender; drain.

Heat oil in large non-stick pan; cook octopus, in batches, until browned all over and just tender. Return octopus to pan with reserved marinade, pasta and parsley; stir over heat until sauce boils.

Per serving fat 7g; kJ 936

steak with

honey, thyme and mustard glaze

1 teaspoon olive oil

4 New York-style beef steaks (600g)

2 tablespoons honey

1/3 cup (80ml) lemon juice

2 teaspoons chopped fresh thyme

1 tablespoon seeded mustard

1 clove garlic, crushed

Heat oil in large non-stick pan; cook beef until browned both sides and cooked as desired. Remove from pan, cover to keep warm.
Add remaining ingredients to same pan; simmer, uncovered, until mixture thickens. Serve glaze over steaks.

Per serving fat 7g; kJ 936

tandoori
lamb pizza

3 lamb fillets (240g),
sliced finely

1¹/₂ tablespoons
tandoori paste

¹/₂ cup (125ml) low-fat
yogurt

1 medium brown onion
(150g), sliced

1 clove garlic, crushed

250g spinach, trimmed

1 tablespoon lemon
juice

335g pizza base

¹/₂ cup (50g) grated
reduced-fat mozzarella
cheese

¹/₂ teaspoon ground
cumin

2 teaspoons water

2 tablespoons fresh
coriander leaves

¹/₂ Lebanese
cucumber chopped

1 small tomato (130g),
chopped

1 tablespoon unsalted
roasted peanuts

Mix lamb with combined paste and half the yogurt in small bowl. Cover;
refrigerate 10 minutes.

Cook lamb, in batches, in large heated non-stick pan, stirring, until
browned all over. Drain on absorbent paper. Cook onion and garlic in
same pan, stirring, until onion is soft. Add spinach and half the lemon
juice; cook, stirring, until spinach just wilts.

Place pizza base on oven tray; sprinkle with cheese, top with spinach
mixture and lamb. Bake, uncovered, in hot oven about 15 minutes or until
just browned and base is crisp.

Meanwhile, whisk cumin and water with remaining juice and yogurt in
small bowl; stir in half the coriander.

Sprinkle remaining coriander and combined remaining ingredients over
pizza; serve with yogurt cumin sauce.

Per serving fat 8.2g; kJ 987

44 fajita-style
lamb

8 lamb fillets (640g), sliced

2 tablespoons lime juice

2 cloves garlic, crushed

1 tablespoon drained chopped jalapeno chillies

2 tablespoons chopped fresh coriander leaves

cooking oil spray

2 medium brown onions (300g), sliced

2 small red capsicums (300g), sliced

2 small yellow capsicums (300g), sliced

4 x 24cm round tortillas

½ cup (125ml) bottled mild salsa

Combine lamb with juice, garlic, chilli and coriander in bowl. Cover; refrigerate 10 minutes. Coat large non-stick pan with cooking oil spray, heat pan; cook onion and capsicum, stirring, until soft. Remove onion mixture from pan, cover to keep warm. Cook lamb, in batches, in same pan, stirring, until browned all over and cooked as desired; cover to keep warm.

Wrap stacked tortillas in foil, place on oven tray; heat in moderate oven about 10 minutes.

Place onion mixture, lamb and salsa along centre of each tortilla, roll up to enclose filling.

Per serving fat 10.8g;
kJ 1727

tomato, spinach and pasta
salad

14 medium egg tomatoes (1kg), halved

2 tablespoons balsamic vinegar

2 cloves garlic, crushed

$^1/_3$ cup chopped fresh oregano leaves

375g penne

1 tablespoon Dijon mustard

1 cup (250ml) buttermilk

150g reduced-fat fetta cheese, crumbled

150g baby spinach leaves

Place tomatoes, cut side up, on wire rack in baking dish. Brush tomatoes with combined vinegar, garlic and half the oregano; bake, uncovered, in hot oven 20 minutes or until soft.

Cook pasta in large pan of boiling water, uncovered, until just tender; drain. Rinse; drain well.

Blend or process 8 of the tomato halves with mustard, buttermilk and remaining oregano until smooth.

Combine the remaining tomatoes, pasta, buttermilk mixture, cheese and spinach in large bowl; mix gently.

Per serving fat 8.5g; kJ 2067

46 tuna **bean**

salad

425g can tuna in brine, drained, flaked

400g can cannellini beans, rinsed, drained

100g mesclun

1 small red onion (100g), sliced

3 small tomatoes (400g), seeded, sliced

1/2 cup (125ml) bottled no-oil French salad dressing

Combine all ingredients in large bowl; mix gently.

Per serving 2.6g; kJ 799

moroccan

minted beef

1 teaspoon vegetable oil

750g beef strips

1 large brown onion (200g), sliced

2 teaspoons ground cumin

1 teaspoon grated lemon rind

400g can tomatoes

2 tablespoons slivered almonds, toasted

2 teaspoons finely shredded fresh mint leaves

Heat oil in large non-stick pan; cook beef, in batches, until browned all over and cooked as desired.

Cook onion in same pan, stirring until soft. Add cumin and rind; cook, stirring, until fragrant. Stir in undrained crushed tomatoes; simmer, uncovered, stirring occasionally, about 5 minutes or until mixture thickens slightly. Return beef to pan with nuts and mint; stir until hot.

Per serving fat 12g; kJ 1277

chickpea and zucchini

tagine

cooking oil spray

1 medium brown onion (150g), sliced

1 clove garlic, crushed

1 teaspoon ground turmeric

1/2 teaspoon ground cinnamon

1/2 teaspoon ground ginger

600g pumpkin, chopped

4 large zucchini (600g), chopped

300g small yellow squash, chopped

1 litre (4 cups) vegetable stock

1 tablespoon honey

3/4 cup (155g) chopped, seeded prunes

2 x 300g cans chickpeas, rinsed, drained

1/3 cup chopped fresh coriander leaves

lemon couscous

2 cups (400g) couscous

2 cups (500ml) boiling water

1 tablespoon grated lemon rind

2 tablespoons flaked almonds

Coat large non-stick pan with cooking oil spray, heat pan; cook onion and garlic, stirring, until onion is soft. Add spices; stir until fragrant. Add vegetables, stock, honey and prunes; simmer, covered, about 20 minutes or until vegetables are just tender. Stir in chickpeas and coriander; simmer, uncovered, until hot. Serve with Lemon Couscous.

Lemon Couscous Place couscous in heatproof bowl; cover with the water. Stand 5 minutes, fluff with fork. Heat large non-stick pan; cook rind and nuts, stirring constantly, until nuts are browned lightly. Add couscous; stir until hot.

Per serving fat 9.2g; kJ 2847

50 pasta with veal and broad beans

250g rigatoni

300g frozen broad beans

750g veal steaks, sliced

600ml jar tomato pasta sauce

1/2 cup (60g) seeded black olives, sliced

1/3 cup (25g) flaked parmesan cheese

Cook pasta in large pan of boiling water, uncovered, until just tender; drain.

Cook broad beans in large pan of boiling water, uncovered, 1 minute, drain; peel.

Cook veal in large heated non-stick pan, in batches, until browned all over. Return veal to pan with sauce, beans and olives; stir over heat until hot. Toss sauce through pasta; sprinkle with the cheese.

Per serving fat 10.3g; kJ 2471

marinated steaks 51

with peach salsa

cooking oil spray

4 beef eye fillet steaks (600g)

¹/₃ cup (80ml) mint jelly

2 tablespoons balsamic vinegar

5 large fresh peaches, (1kg) chopped

3 small fresh red chillies, seeded, chopped finely

Coat grill pan with cooking oil spray, heat pan; char-grill (or grill or barbecue) beef until browned on both sides and cooked as desired.

Combine jelly and vinegar in small pan; simmer, uncovered, until thickened slightly. Serve steaks with mint jelly mixture and combined peaches and chilli. Serve steaks with rocket leaves, if desired.

Per serving fat 7.3g; kJ 1389

52 fettuccine

with tuna and olives

500g fettuccine

425g can tuna in brine, drained

2 medium tomatoes (380g), chopped

1/2 cup (60g) seeded black olives, halved

2 teaspoons chopped fresh dill

1/2 cup (125ml) bottled no-oil French salad dressing

Cook pasta in large pan of boiling water, uncovered, until just tender; drain and set aside.

Combine tuna, tomato, olives, dill and dressing in bowl. Combine tuna mixture with pasta in large pan; toss gently over heat until hot.

Per serving fat 7.3g; kJ 2429

hoi sin pork

with green beans

1 teaspoon sesame oil

2 pork fillets (500g), sliced thinly

1 small fresh red chilli, seeded, chopped finely

1 teaspoon grated fresh ginger

1 clove garlic, crushed

2 tablespoons hoi sin sauce

1 small leek (200g), chopped

250g green beans, sliced

2 teaspoons fish sauce

1 teaspoon cornflour

1/2 cup (125ml) chicken stock

Heat oil in large non-stick pan; cook combined pork, chilli, ginger, garlic and hoi sin sauce, in batches, until pork is cooked through.

Cook leek and beans in same pan, stirring, 2 minutes. Return pork to pan with fish sauce and blended cornflour and stock; stir over heat until sauce boils and thickens.

Per serving fat 4.1g; kJ 798

54 beef sukiyaki

100g vermicelli

1/4 cup (60ml) mirin

1 cup (250ml) low-salt soy sauce

1/2 cup (125ml) water

1 tablespoon sugar

1 teaspoon peanut oil

400g beef rump steak, sliced thinly

1 clove garlic, crushed

1 medium carrot (120g), sliced

150g oyster mushrooms

150g shimeji mushrooms

60g enoki mushrooms

125g firm tofu, chopped

125g bok choy, chopped roughly

1/2 small Chinese cabbage (200g), shredded

1/4 cup (50g) canned drained bamboo shoots, sliced

2 green onions, chopped

Place vermicelli in heatproof bowl, cover with hot water; stand 20 minutes or until tender. Drain vermicelli; cut into short lengths.

Combine mirin, sauce, water and sugar in small pan; boil, uncovered, until thickened slightly.

Heat oil in large non-stick pan; cook combined beef and garlic, in batches, until browned all over.

Cook carrot and mushrooms in same pan, stirring, 1 minute. Add tofu, bok choy and cabbage; cook, stirring gently, until cabbage wilts.

Return beef to pan with vermicelli, mirin mixture, bamboo shoots and onion; cook, stirring gently, until hot.

Per serving fat 6g; kJ 1384

56 pork with sun-dried tomato
crust

½ cup (75g) drained sun-dried tomatoes in oil

4 pork butterfly steaks (500g)

red onion salsa

1 medium red onion (170g), chopped

¼ cup (60ml) balsamic vinegar

2 small fresh red chillies, seeded, chopped

2 medium tomatoes (380g), chopped

1 tablespoon chopped fresh sage

2 teaspoons grated lime rind

2 tablespoons lime juice

2 teaspoons sugar

Rinse sun-dried tomatoes under hot water; pat dry with absorbent paper. Process tomatoes until finely chopped; spread over pork.

Cover; refrigerate 10 minutes.

Cook pork in large heated non-stick pan until browned both sides and cooked through. Serve with Red Onion Salsa.

Red Onion Salsa Combine all ingredients in bowl; mix well.

Per serving fat 6.7g; kJ 1058

bucatini with

pancetta and tomato sauce

500g bucatini

1 teaspoon olive oil

1 large brown onion
(200g), chopped

150g pancetta,
chopped

3 x 400g cans
tomatoes, drained,
chopped

1/2 cup (75g) pimiento-
stuffed green olives,
sliced

1/4 cup (20g) flaked
romano cheese

Cook pasta in large
pan of boiling water,
uncovered, until just
tender; drain.

Heat oil in large non-
stick pan; cook onion
and pancetta, stirring,
until onion is soft. Add
tomato; simmer,
covered, 10 minutes
or until sauce thickens
slightly. Add olives;
mix well. Serve sauce
over pasta, top
with cheese.

Per serving fat 8.4g;
kJ 2341

58 pasta with tomato sauce
and mussels

800g small mussels

1 teaspoon olive oil

1 large brown onion (200g), chopped

2 cloves garlic, crushed

1 small fresh red chilli, seeded, chopped

3 x 400g cans tomatoes

1/4 cup (60ml) tomato paste

1 teaspoon sugar

1/3 cup shredded fresh basil leaves

1/2 cup (125ml) fish stock

500g penne

Scrub mussels, remove beards.

Heat oil in large non-stick pan; cook onion and garlic, stirring, until onion is soft. Add chilli, undrained crushed tomatoes, paste, sugar, basil and stock; simmer, uncovered, about 15 minutes or until thickened. Add mussels; simmer, covered, about 5 minutes or until mussels open; discard any unopened mussels.

Cook pasta in large pan of boiling water, uncovered, until just tender; drain well.

Toss hot pasta with tomato mussel sauce.

Per serving fat 3.3g; kJ 2907

orange marmalade pork with
hokkien noodles

500g Hokkien noodles

3 pork fillets (750g), sliced

1/3 cup (115g) orange marmalade

1 clove garlic, crushed

1 tablespoon finely grated fresh ginger

cooking oil spray

1 medium brown onion (150g), sliced

500g baby bok choy, trimmed

1/4 cup (60ml) hoi sin sauce

1/4 cup (60ml) plum sauce

Rinse noodles in hot water; drain.

Combine pork, marmalade, garlic and ginger in bowl. Cover; refrigerate 10 minutes.

Coat large non-stick pan with cooking oil spray, heat pan; cook undrained pork and onion, in batches, until pork is browned all over and cooked through.

Return pork and onion to pan with noodles and remaining ingredients; cook, stirring, until the sauce boils and thickens.

Per serving fat 6g; kJ 2137

glossary

bacon rashers also known as slices of bacon.

streaky bacon: the fatty end of a bacon rasher without the lean (eye) meat.

bean sprouts also known as bean shoots.

beef

eye-fillet: tenderloin.

minced: also known as ground beef.

New York-style steak: sirloin without T-bone.

rump steak: boneless tender cut.

scotch fillet: eye of the rib roast; rib-eye roll; cube roll.

strips: strips prepared from blade, fillet, rib-eye, round, rump, sirloin and topside.

black bean sauce a Chinese sauce made from fermented soy beans.

bok choy also called pak choi or Chinese white cabbage; baby bok choy is also available.

breadcrumbs

wholemeal stale: 1- or 2-day-old wholemeal bread made into crumbs by grating, blending or processing.

burghul also known as bulghur wheat; hulled steamed and crushed wheat kernels.

buttermilk low-fat milk cultured to give a slightly sour, tangy taste; low-fat yogurt can be substituted.

Cajun seasoning packaged blend can include paprika, basil, onion, fennel, thyme, cayenne and tarragon.

cheese

reduced-fat fetta: we used a fetta with an average fat content of 15 per cent.

low-fat mozzarella: we used reduced fat mozzarella

chicken, tenderloin thin strip of meat lying just under the breast.

Chinese broccoli also known as gai lum.

Chinese cabbage also known as Peking cabbage or Napa cabbage.

choy sum also known as flowering bok choy or flowering white cabbage.

coconut milk powder coconut milk that has been dehydrated and ground to a fine powder.

couscous: a fine, grain-like cereal product.

fish

white fillet: means non-oily fish. this category includes bream, flathead, whiting, snapper, jewfish and ling fish pieces that have been boned and skinned.

fish sauce also called nam pla or nuoc nam; made from pulverised salted fermented fish; use sparingly.

garam masala a blend of cardamom, cinnamon, cloves, coriander, fennel and cumin, roasted and ground together.

garlic chives have a stronger flavour than chives.

hoisin sauce a thick Chinese paste made from salted fermented soy beans.

hummus a Middle-Eastern dip made from pureed chickpeas, tahini, garlic and lemon juice.

ketjap manis Indonesian sweet, thick soy sauce which has sugar and spices added.

kumara Polynesian name for orange-fleshed sweet potato.

marinara mix a mixture of uncooked, chopped seafood available from fishmongers.

mesclun a mixture of assorted lettuce and other green leaves.

mirin a sweet low-alcohol rice wine used in Japanese cooking; sometimes referred to simply as rice wine but should not be confused with sake, the Japanese rice wine made for drinking.

mushrooms

button: small, cultivated white mushrooms having a delicate, subtle flavour.

enoki: slender, 10cm-long body with a tiny head, it is creamy-yellow in colour and crisp in texture. sold in clumps, it has a mild flavour and is good in stir-fries.

oyster (abalone): grey-white fan-shaped mushroom.

shimeji: grey in colour with a rich spicy flavour; good eaten in salads.

noodles

fresh egg: made from wheat flour and eggs; strands vary in thickness.

fresh rice: thick, wide, almost white in colour; made from rice and vegetable oil. Must be covered with boiling water to remove starch and excess oil before using.

hokkien: also known as stir-fry noodles; fresh wheat flour noodles resembling thick, yellow-brown spaghetti needing no pre-cooking before being used.

oil

cooking oil spray: vegetable oil in an aerosol can.

olive: mono-unsaturated; made from the pressing of tree-ripened olives. Light olive oil describes the mild flavour, not the fat levels.

peanut: pressed from ground peanuts; most commonly used oil in Asian cooking because of its high smoke point.

sesame: made from roasted, crushed, white sesame seeds; a flavouring rather than a cooking medium.

vegetable: any of a number of oils sourced from plants rather than animal fats.

onion

green: also known as scallion or (incorrectly) shallot; an immature onion picked before the bulb has formed, having a long, bright-green edible stalk.

red: a sweet-flavoured, large, purple-red onion, good eaten raw in salads.

oyster sauce rich, brown sauce, made from oysters and their brine, cooked with salt and soy sauce.

pancetta an Italian salt-cured pork roll, usually cut from the belly; bacon can be substituted.

plum sauce a thick, sweet and sour dipping sauce made from plums, vinegar, sugar, chillies and spices.

polenta a flour-like cereal made of ground corn (maize); similar to cornmeal but coarser and darker in colour; also the name of the dish made from it.

potatoes, kipfler finger-length, light-brown skinned, nutty flavoured potato, good baked or in salads.

pork

butterfly: skinless, boneless mid-loin chop, split in half and flattened.

fillet: skinless, boneless eye-fillet cut from the loin.

schnitzel: is usually cut from the leg or rump.

rice

arborio: small, round grain rice well-suited to absorb a large amount of liquid; use to make risotto.

long-grain: elongated grain, remains separate when cooked; most popular steaming rice in Asia.

short-grain: fat, almost round grain with a high starch content; clumps together when cooked.

saffron

available in strands or ground form; imparts a yellow-orange colour to food once infused.

sambal oelek (also ulek or olek) Indonesian salty paste made from ground chillies.

silverbeet also known as Swiss chard.

snow peas also called mange tout ("eat all").

snow pea sprouts sprouted seeds of the snow pea.

tabasco sauce brand name of an extremely fiery sauce made from vinegar, hot red peppers and salt.

tat soi also known as rosette pak choy, a tender variety of bok choy.

tofu also known as bean curd, made from the "milk" of crushed soy beans; comes fresh as soft or firm, and processed as fried or pressed dried sheets. Leftover fresh tofu can be refrigerated in water (which is changed daily) up to 4 days. Silken tofu refers to the method by which it is made —where it is strained through silk.

tortilla thin, round unleavened bread originating in Mexico. Two kinds are available: made from wheat flour and corn (maizemeal).

These conversions are approximate only, but the difference between an exact and the approximate conversion of various liquid and dry measures is minimal and will not affect your cooking results.

Note: NZ, Canada, USA and UK all use 15ml tablespoons. Australian tablespoons measure 20ml.

All cup and spoon measurements are level.

Measuring equipment

The difference between one country's measuring cups and another's is, at most, within a 2 or 3 teaspoon variance. (For the record, 1 Australian metric measuring cup holds approximately 250ml.) The most accurate way of measuring dry ingredients is to weigh them. For liquids, use a clear glass or plastic jug having metric markings.

How to measure

When using graduated measuring cups, shake dry ingredients loosely into the appropriate cup. Do not tap the cup on a bench or tightly pack the ingredients unless directed to do so. Level the top of measuring cups and measuring spoons with a knife. When measuring liquids, place a clear glass or plastic jug having metric markings on a flat surface to check accuracy at eye level.

Dry Measures

metric	imperial
15g	1/2oz
30g	1oz
60g	2oz
90g	3oz
125g	4oz (1/4lb)
155g	5oz
185g	6oz
220g	7oz
250g	8oz (1/2lb)
280g	9oz
315g	10oz
345g	11oz
375g	12oz (3/4lb)
410g	13oz
440g	14oz
470g	15oz
500g	16oz (1lb)
750g	24oz (11/2lb)
1kg	32oz (2lb)

We use large eggs having an average weight of 60g.

Liquid Measures

metric	imperial
30ml	1 fluid oz
60ml	2 fluid oz
100ml	3 fluid oz
125ml	4 fluid oz
150ml	5 fluid oz (1/4 pint/1 gill)
190ml	6 fluid oz
250ml (1cup)	8 fluid oz
300ml	10 fluid oz (1/2 pint)
500ml	16 fluid oz
600ml	20 fluid oz (1 pint)
1000ml (1litre)	13/4 pints

Helpful Measures

metric	imperial
3mm	1/8in
6mm	1/4in
1cm	1/2in
2cm	3/4in
2.5cm	1in
6cm	21/2in
8cm	3in
20cm	8in
23cm	9in
25cm	10in
30cm	12in (1ft)

Oven Temperatures

These oven temperatures are only a guide. Always check the manufacturer's manual.

	°C (Celsius)	°F (Fahrenheit)	Gas Mark
Very slow	120	250	1
Slow	150	300	2
Moderately slow	160	325	3
Moderate	180 –190	350 – 375	4
Moderately hot	200 – 210	400 – 425	5
Hot	220 – 230	450 – 475	6
Very hot	240 – 250	500 – 525	7

at your fingertips

These elegant slipcovers store up to 10 mini books and make the books instantly accessible.

And the metric measuring cups and spoons make following our recipes a piece of cake.

Book Holder
Australia and overseas:
$A8.95 (incl. GST).

Metric Measuring Set
Australia: $6.50 (incl. GST).
New Zealand: $A8.00.
Elsewhere: $A9.95.
Prices include postage
and handling.
This offer is available
in all countries.

Photocopy and complete the coupon below

Mail or fax Photocopy and complete the coupon below and post to ACP Books Reader Offer, ACP Publishing, GPO Box 4967, Sydney NSW 2001, *or* fax to (02) 9267 4967.

Phone Have your credit card details ready, then phone 136 116 (Mon-Fri, 8.00am - 6.00pm; Sat 8.00am - 6.00pm).

Australian residents We accept the credit cards listed on the coupon, money orders and cheques.

Overseas residents We accept the credit cards listed on the coupon, drafts in $A drawn on an Australian bank, and also British, New Zealand and U.S. cheques in the currency of the country of issue.

☐ **Book holder**   ☐ **Metric measuring set**
Please indicate number(s) required.

Mr/Mrs/Ms _____

Address _____

_____

Postcode _____ Country _____

Phone: Business hours ( ) _____

I enclose my cheque/money order for $_____ payable to ACP Publishing

OR: please charge $ _____ to my: ☐ Bankcard ☐ Visa

☐ Amex ☐ MasterCard ☐ Diners Club Expiry Date ___/___

Cardholder's signature _____

Please allow up to 30 days for delivery within Australia.

Allow up to 6 weeks for overseas deliveries. Both offers expire 31/12/02.
HLLF02

Food director Pamela Clark
Assistant food editor Kathy McGarry

ACP BOOKS STAFF
Editorial director Susan Tomnay
Creative Director Hieu Nguyen
Senior editor Julie Collard
Concept design Jackie Richards
Designer Jackie Richards
Publishing manager (sales) Jennifer McDor
Publishing manager (rights & new titles)
Jane Hazell
Assistant brand manager Donna Gianniotis
Production manager Carol Currie

Publisher Sue Wannan
Group publisher Jill Baker
Chief executive officer John Alexander

Produced by ACP Books, Sydney.

Colour separations by
ACP Colour Graphics Pty Ltd, Sydney.
Printing by Dai Nippon Printing in Hong Kong

Published by ACP Publishing Pty Limited,
54 Park St, Sydney; GPO Box 4088, Sydney,
NSW 1028. Ph: (02) 9282 8618
Fax: (02) 9267 9438.
acpbooks@acp.com.au
www.acpbooks.com.au

To order books phone 136 116.
Send recipe enquiries to
Recipeenquiries@acp.com.au

Australia Distributed by Network Services,
GPO Box 4088, Sydney, NSW 1028.
Ph: (02) 9282 8777 Fax: (02) 9264 3278.

United Kingdom Distributed by Australian
Consolidated Press (UK), Moulton Park Busin
Centre, Red House Road, Moulton Park,
Northampton, NN3 6AQ. Ph: (01604) 497 531
Fax: (01604) 497 533 acpukltd@aol.com

Canada Distributed by Whitecap Books Ltd,
351 Lynn Ave, North Vancouver, BC, V7J 2C4
Ph: (604) 980 9852.

New Zealand Distributed by Netlink Distributic
Company, Level 4, 23 Hargreaves St,
College Hill, Auckland 1, Ph: (9) 302 7616.

South Africa Distributed by
PSD Promotions (Pty) Ltd, PO Box 1175,
Isando 1600, SA, Ph: (011) 392 6065.

Clark, Pamela.
Low-fat food

Includes index.
ISBN 186396 145 3

1. Low-fat cookery – Recipes.
I Title: Australian Women's Weekly..
(Series: Australian Women's Weekly
Healthy Eating mini series).

641.568

© ACP Publishing Pty Limited 1999
ABN 18 053 273 546

This publication is copyright. No part of it may
reproduced or transmitted in any form without
written permission of the publishers.

First published 1999. Reprinted 2001, 2002.

The information about fats on page 3 was con
by nutritionist and dietitian Catherine Saxelby.

Cover: Veal Pizzaiola, page 25, served with
Pan-fried Lemon Vegetables, page 32.
Stylist Jane Collins
Photographer Scott Cameron
Back cover: Cajun Chicken, page 38